299

Young People's Stories of Cooperation

Cooperation is...listening to the ideas of others.

Cooperation is...working together to get things done.

Cooperation is...respecting each person's job as important.

Cooperation is...doing your fair share of the work.

Cooperation is...giving what you do best to help the group.

Compiled by
Henry and Melissa Billings

Young People's Press
San Diego

Editorial, design and production by
Book Production Systems, Inc.

Cover illustration by Jeff Severn.

Published in the United States of America.

2 3 4 5 6 7 8 9 – 99 98 97 96 95
ISBN 1-57279-007-5

Young People's
Stories
of
Cooperation

The Ruler of the Trees

This story comes from Armenia. It starts with an argument. Read to find out how cooperation is used to solve the argument.

One day, long ago, the trees had an argument. They could not decide who among them should be the ruler. Some said it should be the palm tree, since she was so tall and produced such sweet fruit.

But the honeysuckle objected. "My beauty makes people happy," he said. "I should be the ruler."

And the fig tree said, "My fruit is sweet to the taste. I should be the ruler."

And the buckthorn said, "I am sharp and can punish others. I should rule."

3

The palm tree saw that each of these trees would not agree to be ruled by anyone else. But she thought of a plan that might change their minds. "Tell me why I should not be the ruler," she said.

The three trees gave their opinion. "You are indeed very tall and give good fruit," they said. "But you are not easy to grow. You take too long to produce fruit. Because you are so tall, your fruits are hard to reach. And besides, you do not have the special talents we have."

"Very well," said the palm tree. "To overcome these problems, I shall make you part of the royal court in my kingdom."

And so she gave each tree a special job. The beautiful honeysuckle was put in charge of entertainment. The fig tree, oozing sweetness, was asked to work out government problems. The prickly buckthorn was made Chief of Police.

The palm tree gave jobs to all the other trees as well. She put the cedar tree in charge of building. She put the brushwood in charge of heating. She put the brambles in charge of the prisons.

The kingdom ran smoothly, and all the trees were content. And so, you see, no one can rise to power without the cooperation of others.

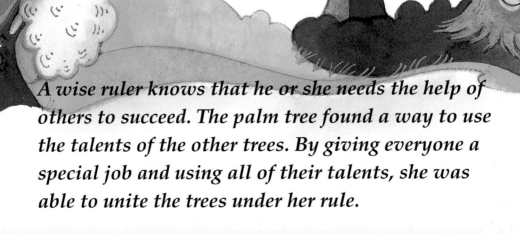

A wise ruler knows that he or she needs the help of others to succeed. The palm tree found a way to use the talents of the other trees. By giving everyone a special job and using all of their talents, she was able to unite the trees under her rule.

The Animals Who Set Up Housekeeping

This story comes from Norway. The characters are five different animals. How do you suppose they could work together to build a safe house in the woods?

Once upon a time there was a sheep on a farm. Every day she was fattened up with plenty of good food. One day the farmer brought her even more food than usual. "Eat away, sheep," the farmer said, "for you won't be here much longer. Tomorrow we are going to kill you and turn you into winter food."

The sheep was scared. After the farmer left, the sheep ate all of the food and then butted out the door of her pen. She hurried away to the neighboring farm. There she went to see a pig who was a friend of hers.

9

"Pig!" cried the sheep. "Do you know why it is you are so well off? Do you know why they fatten you and take such good care of you?"

"No, I don't," said the pig.

"Well, I know. They are going to kill you and eat you!" said the sheep.

"Are they?" cried the pig. "What shall I do?"

"Come with me," said the sheep. "We'll go off to the woods and build ourselves a new home."

The pig agreed. Quickly the two set off. Soon they met a goose.

"Good day," said the goose. "Where are you two going in such a hurry?"

"Good day," the sheep answered. "We are going to set up a home for ourselves in the woods."

"Well," said the goose, "I should like a home of my own, too. May I go with you?"

"What can you do to help?" asked the pig.

"I can pluck moss and stuff it into the seams between the boards," the goose replied. "That way the house will be tight and warm."

Above all things, piggy wished to be warm and comfortable. So he told the goose he could join them.

When they had gone a bit farther, they met a rabbit, who came frisking out of the woods.

"Good day," she said. "How far are you trotting today?"

"Good day. We are going deep into the woods to build ourselves a house," said the sheep. "For you know, there is nothing like a home."

"I have often thought of that myself," said the rabbit. "I have half a mind to go with you."

The pig laughed. "If we ever get into trouble we might use you to scare away the wolves. But I don't think you would be any help to us in building a house."

"Don't make fun of me," said the rabbit. "I have teeth to gnaw pegs and paws to drive them into the wall. I would make a fine carpenter."

So the sheep, pig, and goose agreed to let the rabbit join them. When they had gone a bit farther, they met a rooster.

"Good day. Where are you going today?" the rooster asked.

"Good day. We are going off to the woods to build ourselves a house," said the sheep. "It is good to travel east and west, but after all a home is best."

"Yes," said the rooster. "You are right. And if you agree, I would like to come with you."

"Hold on!" said the pig. "How can you help us?"

"Well," said the rooster, "what would you do without a rooster? I am up early, and I wake every one."

"Very true," said the pig. "Sleep is the biggest thief of all. He steals half of one's life. Come along and protect us from him."

So they all set off into the woods together to build a house. The pig knocked down trees to make logs.

The sheep dragged the logs into place.

The rabbit hammered the logs together. The goose plucked moss and stuffed it into the seams. The rooster made sure no one slept too late in the morning.

Soon the house was ready. There the five animals lived in peace and were merry and well.

The pig and the sheep were wise to let the other animals join them. None of the animals could have built a house alone, but by working together they were able to do it.

The MOUSE, the BIRD, and the SAUSAGE

This story comes from Germany. Read to find out what happens when one roommate decides he no longer wants to cooperate.

Once upon a time a mouse and a bird and a sausage lived together in perfect peace. It was the bird's job to fly to the forest every day and bring back wood. The mouse fetched the water, made the fire, and set the table. And the sausage did the cooking. He flavored the food by jumping right into the pot and stirring it three times.

One day when the bird was out gathering wood, he met a squirrel. The bird told the squirrel about his wonderful life. The squirrel laughed. She said, "You are a fool to do so much work while the mouse and the sausage lead such easy lives."

The bird decided she was right. When he got home, he announced that he would no longer fetch the wood. The mouse and the sausage tried to reason with him. But he would not listen.

At last they drew straws to divide the work differently. It ended up that the sausage was to fetch wood. The mouse was to do the cooking. The bird was to draw water and make the fire.

The next day, the sausage went out to gather wood. The
bird and the mouse waited for him to come home. They waited
a long time. But the sausage did not return. Finally, the bird
flew off to look for him.

In the woods, the bird met a dog. The dog had seen the
sausage and had thought he would make a tasty dinner. So the
dog had eaten him!

Sadly, the bird took up the wood and carried it home himself. He told the mouse what he had learned. They were both very troubled, but decided they should make the best of things. They wanted to stay together. So while the bird set the table, the mouse prepared the food.

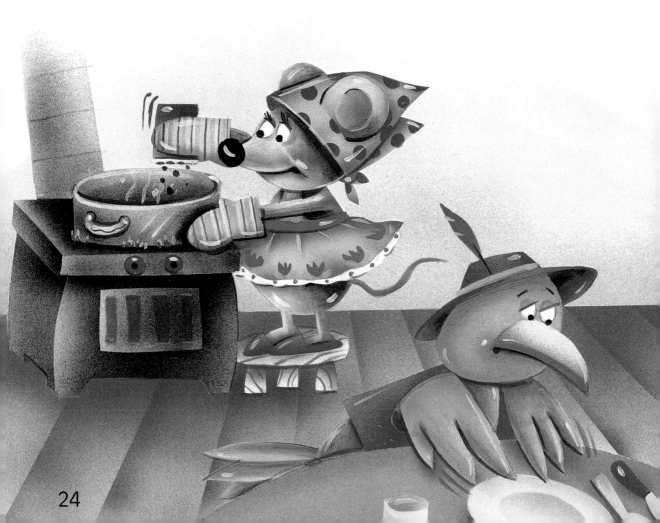

When it was time to flavor the soup, the mouse climbed into the pot just as the sausage had always done. But the mouse was not a sausage. She could not stand the heat and hot water. In just an instant, she died.

When the bird came to dish up his dinner, he did not see the mouse anywhere. He looked and looked for her. In his search, he turned over the heap of wood on the floor. The wood caught fire. Quickly the bird went to fetch water to put it out. But the bird dropped the bucket in the well. When he tried to get it, he fell in. He could not get out again. And so he, like the mouse and the sausage, came to an unhappy end.

At the beginning of the story, the bird, the mouse, and the sausage were cooperating nicely. They had a wonderful life together. But after talking to the squirrel, the bird felt cheated. He no longer appreciated the work done by the mouse and the sausage. He forgot that each friend was doing what he or she did best. The bird demanded a change. He refused to listen when his friends tried to reason with him. As a result, they all ended up with jobs they couldn't handle.

This story comes from China. It reminds us that each person has a part to play in the success of family, school, and community. What is your part?

HOLDING UP THE SKY

One day an elephant saw a hummingbird lying flat on its back on the ground.
The bird's tiny feet were raised up into the air.

"What on earth are you doing, Hummingbird?" asked the elephant.

The hummingbird replied,
"I have heard that the sky might fall today.
If that should happen,
I am ready to do my bit in holding it up."

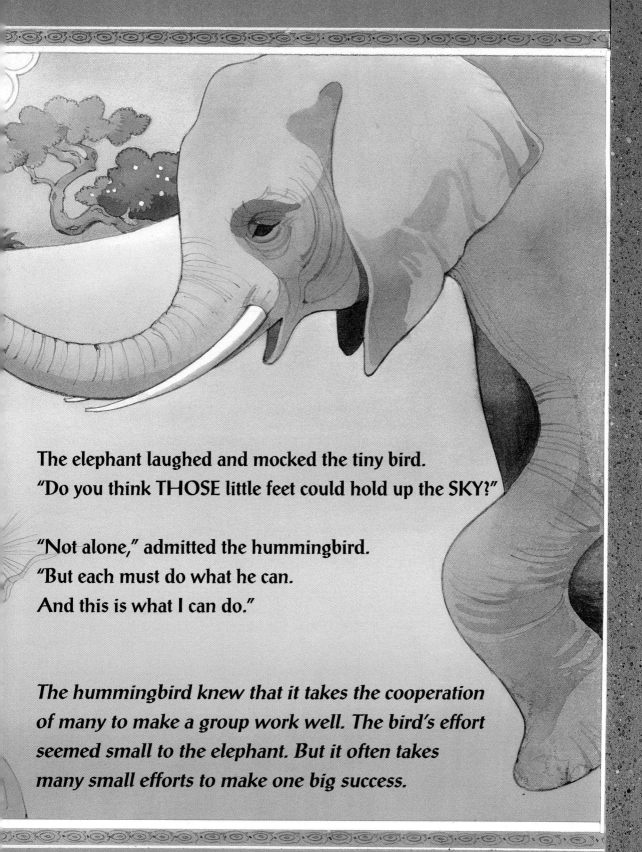

The elephant laughed and mocked the tiny bird.
"Do you think THOSE little feet could hold up the SKY?"

"Not alone," admitted the hummingbird.
"But each must do what he can.
And this is what I can do."

The hummingbird knew that it takes the cooperation of many to make a group work well. The bird's effort seemed small to the elephant. But it often takes many small efforts to make one big success.

Acknowledgments

Grateful acknowledgment is made for permission
to reprint the following copyrighted material:

"Holding Up the Sky" is reprinted by permission from
PEACE TALES: WORLD FOLKTALES TO TALK ABOUT
by Margaret Read MacDonald (Linnet Books: 1992).

"The King of the Trees" adapted and retitled "The
Ruler of the Trees" from ARMENIAN FOLK-TALES
AND FABLES, translated by Charles Downing, 1972.
Reprinted by permission of Oxford University Press.